USING HAND LENSES AND MICROSCOPES

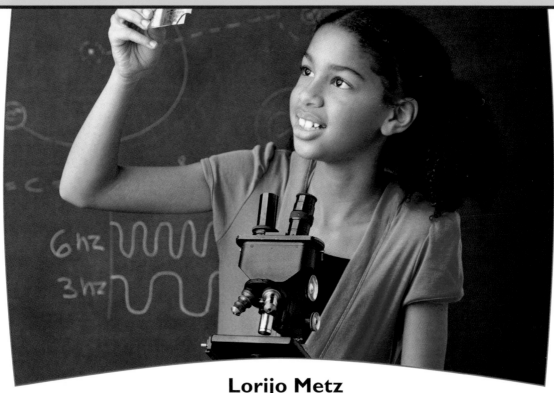

Lorijo Metz

PowerKiDS press.

New York

Dedicated to Lilibette, who magnifies her Grandma Kathleen's happiness tenfold

Published in 2013 by The Rosen Publishing Group, Inc.
29 East 21st Street, New York, NY 10010

First Edition

Editor: Amelie von Zumbusch
Book Design: Kate Laczynski

Photo Credits: Cover Hill Street Studios/Blend Images/Getty Images; p. 4 AISPIX by Image Source/Shutterstock.com; p. 5 (left) Kletr/Shutterstock.com; p. 5 (right) © iStockphoto.com/Oleg Kozlov; p. 6 Rob Marmion/Shutterstock.com; p. 7 Last Refuge/ Robert Harding World Imagery/Getty Images; p. 8 (both) GIPhotoStock/Photo Researchers/Getty Images; p. 9 Milos Luzanin/ Shutterstock.com; p. 11 Szasz-Fabian Ilka Erika/Shutterstock.com; p. 12 Thorsten Schmitt/Shutterstock.com; p. 13 AVAVA/ Shutterstock.com; p. 14 (left) Compassionate Eye Foundation/Tom Grill/Digital Vision/Getty Images; pp. 14 (right), 22 iStockphoto/Thinkstock; p. 15 Lisa F. Young/Shutterstock.com; p. 17 Marco Mayer/Shutterstock.com; p. 18 Noel Hendrickson/ Digital Vision/Getty Images; p. 19 Susumu Nishinaga/Science Photo Library/Getty Images; p. 20 John & Lisa Merrill/ Photographer's Choice RF/Getty Images; p. 21 Peter Mason/Taxi/Getty Images.

Library of Congress Cataloging-in-Publication Data

Metz, Lorijo.
 Using hand lenses and microscopes / by Lorijo Metz. — 1st ed.
    p. cm. — (Science tools)
 Includes index.
 ISBN 978-1-4488-9687-5 (library binding) — ISBN 978-1-4488-9832-9 (pbk.) —
 ISBN 978-1-4488-9833-6 (6-pack)
 1. Microscopy—Juvenile literature. I. Title.
 QH278.M48 2013
 570.28'2—dc23
                          2012030675

Manufactured in the United States of America

CPSIA Compliance Information: Batch #W13PK4: For Further Information contact Rosen Publishing, New York, New York at 1-800-237-9932

CONTENTS

Hand Lenses and Microscopes

Have you ever looked at something small, like a word on a dime or the wing of a butterfly, and wished you could see it better? Using a hand lens or microscope, you can. Hand lenses and microscopes are tools that help you see things better.

Hand lenses are also known as magnifying glasses. They are great for getting a closer look at things that you find in your backyard or at a park.

Microscopes allow us to study things the human eye could never see on its own. Using a microscope, scientists can study tiny human cells to find better ways to treat illnesses. Though not as powerful, hand lenses can be used almost anywhere. You can use them to see bugs in your backyard and much more.

Microscope

Hand lens

Magnification

Hand lenses and microscopes help us see things better by **magnifying** them, or making them appear larger than their normal size. The amount they magnify something, or their magnification, is usually shown by a number with the letter *x* after it. A hand lens that makes things appear two times as large has a magnification of 2x.

The microscope that this girl is using can be set at three different magnification levels.

A hand lens with a magnification of 4x makes objects appear four times larger.

You cannot change the magnification on a hand lens. However, you can change the magnification on most microscopes. Microscopes tend to be more powerful magnifiers than hand lenses are.

This photo of a vine weevil was taken with a powerful microscope.

Light moves in a straight line unless something bends it. A lens is a curved piece of glass or plastic that **refracts**, or bends, light to change the way things look. **Concave** lenses are thin in the middle. They make things look smaller. **Convex** lenses are thicker in the middle.

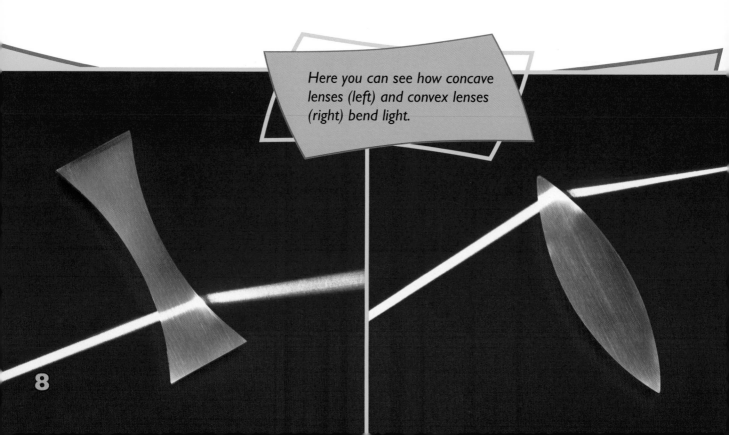

Here you can see how concave lenses (left) and convex lenses (right) bend light.

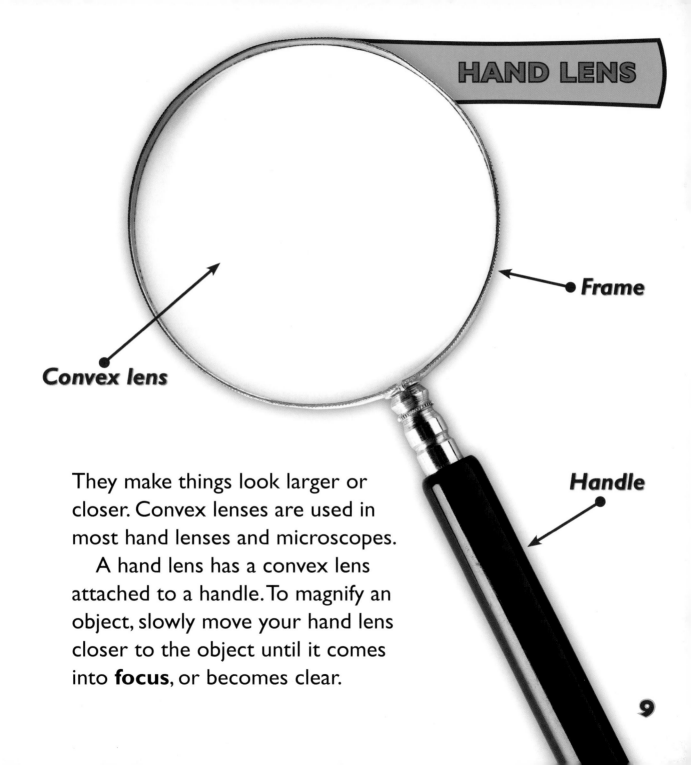

Frame

Convex lens

Handle

They make things look larger or closer. Convex lenses are used in most hand lenses and microscopes.

A hand lens has a convex lens attached to a handle. To magnify an object, slowly move your hand lens closer to the object until it comes into **focus**, or becomes clear.

9

Compound Light Microscopes

Light microscopes use light and lenses to make objects look larger. Many schools use compound light microscopes, which have two or more lenses. One lens is in the **eyepiece** at the top of a tube called a body tube. At the bottom of the body tube are one or more **objective lenses** with different magnifications. Multiple lenses are often on round discs you can turn to select a certain lens.

The microscope's base has a stage with clips to hold a **slide** for viewing. There is often a light or a mirror that reflects light up through a hole in the stage. This makes the slide easier to see.

As you might guess from its name, the eyepiece is the part of a microscope that you look into.

It's exciting to see an object at different magnifications. Two knobs on the microscope arm move the body tube up and down to focus on your object. The coarse-adjustment knob makes large adjustments, while the fine-adjustment knob makes smaller adjustments.

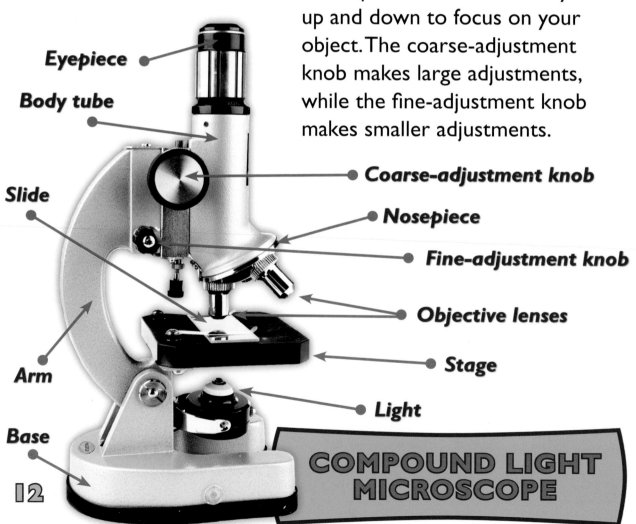

Eyepiece

Body tube

Slide

Arm

Base

Coarse-adjustment knob

Nosepiece

Fine-adjustment knob

Objective lenses

Stage

Light

COMPOUND LIGHT MICROSCOPE

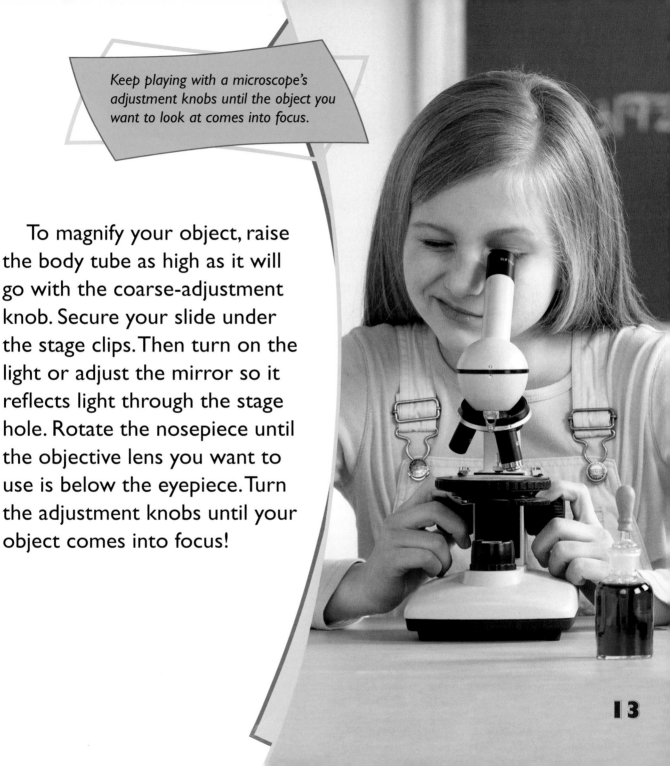

Keep playing with a microscope's adjustment knobs until the object you want to look at comes into focus.

To magnify your object, raise the body tube as high as it will go with the coarse-adjustment knob. Secure your slide under the stage clips. Then turn on the light or adjust the mirror so it reflects light through the stage hole. Rotate the nosepiece until the objective lens you want to use is below the eyepiece. Turn the adjustment knobs until your object comes into focus!

How to Prepare Microscope Slides

Scientists place objects, or **specimens**, on glass rectangles called slides to view them under a microscope. A thin piece of glass or plastic called a cover slip goes on top of the specimen.

Scientists use wet-mount slides for live specimens that need to stay in water. Also, some specimens are easier to see if they are wet.

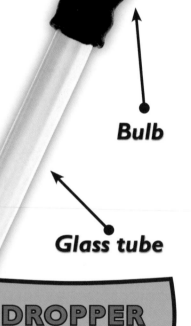

Bulb

Tip

Glass tube

DROPPER

Prepare your slide carefully before placing it on a microscope stage.

To prepare a wet-mount slide, place a dry glass slide on a table. Place your specimen in the center of the slide. If it's not already in liquid, use a dropper to put one drop of water on the specimen. Holding only the edges, carefully place the cover slip on top. Do not press down.

If you want to look at a liquid under a microscope, use a dropper to place the liquid on a slide, as this man is doing.

The Scientific Method

Scientists **observe**, or notice, things around them and question how they work. Based on what they know, they come up with an idea, or **hypothesis**, that tries to answer their question. To test their hypothesis, they create an **experiment**.

Hand lenses and microscopes are good for both observing things and answering questions about things that you might not otherwise be able to see. Take careful notes on everything you do and observe. Scientists write their notes in **logs**. Repeating an experiment several times and comparing the results is the only way to see if your hypothesis is correct.

Good scientists keep good notes. When you are keeping a log, include as many details as you can think of.

17

In 1931, scientists invented the transmission **electron** microscope, or TEM. A TEM fires a stream of very small particles called electrons at an object. With this high-powered microscope, scientists can see things so small you could fit a billion of them in a golf ball. The scanning electron microscope, or SEM, creates a 3-D image, instead of a flat one. It lets scientists see all the sides of an object.

This scientist is working with a scanning electron microscope.

Scanning electron microscopes can take great photos of things that are too small to see with the naked eye. Scientists used an SEM to take this photo of sunflower pollen.

Today, we also have acoustic microscopes. These use sound waves to see through objects. Doctors can use acoustic microscopes to search for cancer inside a body, rather than cutting a patient open.

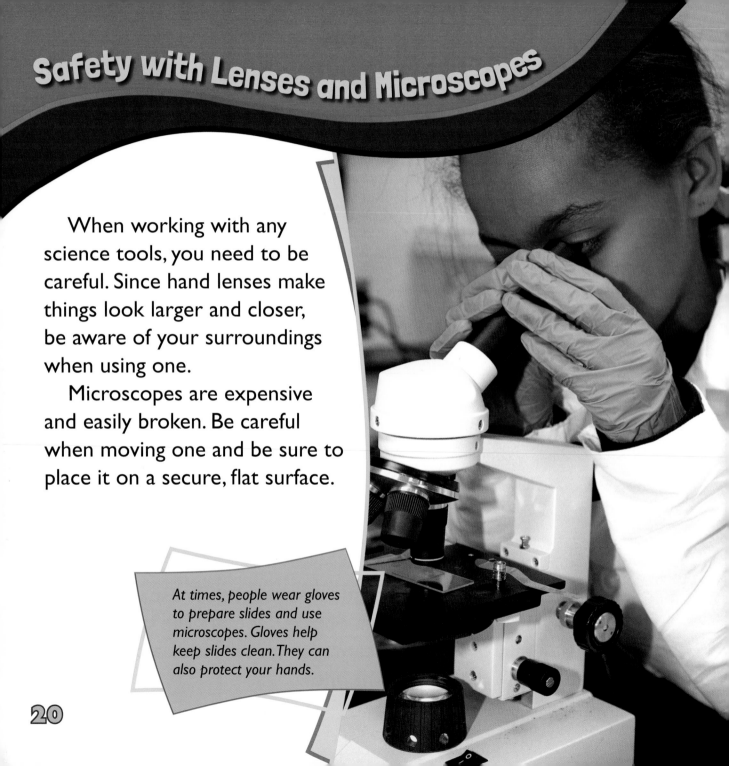

When working with any science tools, you need to be careful. Since hand lenses make things look larger and closer, be aware of your surroundings when using one.

Microscopes are expensive and easily broken. Be careful when moving one and be sure to place it on a secure, flat surface.

At times, people wear gloves to prepare slides and use microscopes. Gloves help keep slides clean. They can also protect your hands.

Cover all slides with cover slips to protect your specimens. When turning lenses, raise the body tube to avoid hitting a lens against the stage or specimen. If you break a microscope part made of glass, such as a lens, cover slip, or slide, ask an adult to help you clean it up.

If you look at bugs or other small animals with a hand lens, be careful not to harm these living things.

TIME TO OBSERVE

In this experiment, you will observe leaves from three trees. You will need:

1. Leaves from three different trees
2. A hand lens
3. A notebook or paper
4. Something to draw with

Draw a picture of each leaf in your notebook or on a piece of paper. Make the drawings as detailed as possible. Next, look at the same three leaves through a hand lens. Draw what you see and then compare the two drawings. What things did you observe using a hand lens that you did not observe using only your eyes? Finally, compare your drawings of the three leaves. How are they the same and how are they different? Are there differences you could observe only using a hand lens?

GLOSSARY

concave (kon-KAYV) Dipping toward the center, like a spoon.

convex (kon-VEKS) Curving outward, like the outside of a bowl.

electron (ih-LEK-tron) The part of the atom that has a negative charge.

experiment (ik-SPER-uh-ment) A set of actions or steps taken to learn more about something.

eyepiece (EYE-pees) The part of a microscope through which people look.

focus (FOH-kis) To make clear.

hypothesis (hy-PAH-theh-ses) A possible answer to a problem.

logs (LOGZ) Records of day-to-day activities.

magnifying (MAG-nuh-fy-ing) Making something look larger than it is.

objective lenses (ub-JEK-tiv LENZ-ez) Curved glasses in a microscope that face the object being looked at.

observe (ub-ZERV) To notice.

refracts (rih-FRAKTS) Changes the direction of a light ray or a sound wave by slowing it down or by bending it away from a straight path.

slide (SLYD) A clear piece of glass or plastic on which people place things to study with a microscope.

specimens (SPES-menz) Samples.

INDEX

WEBSITES

Due to the changing nature of Internet links, PowerKids Press has developed an online list of websites related to the subject of this book. This site is updated regularly. Please use this link to access the list:
www.powerkidslinks.com/scto/lens/